To my strong Boy.

You like a lot of things.

You like to eat your favorite snack foods, like, a box of cereal, cotton candy, a big donut or an ice cream cone stacked to the sky, or a plate of warm chocolate chip cookies. Sometimes I call you a little cookie monster.

But that is not who you are.

You like to play soccer in the front yard and basketball in the living room. You play with puzzles on the living room rug and build the biggest Lego castles in your bedroom. You can do a lot of really cool things.

But that is not who you are.

You play pirates and treasure hunters. You pretend you are a tractor and dig deep holes in the back yard. Next, you are a dinosaur stomping through the house and roaring as loud as can be.

But that is not who you are.

You are not what you eat, or what you
create, or what you can do or what you
can build. And you are not who you
pretend to be.

Let me tell you who you really are.

You are strong and you use your strength to help and then flex your arms and say "Daddy, look!" You are my strong boy.

That is who you are.

You are compassionate and you care for people. When people fall down and get hurt, you pick people up.

That is who you are.

You are generous and kind. You share your toys and make new friends. Everyone is welcome at your lunch table.

That is who you are.

You stand for what is right. You speak up for those who do not know how to speak up for themselves and you defend those who cannot defend themselves. You care about justice. Other kids look up to you and are following in your footsteps.
You are a leader.

That is who you are.

You love people. People who look like you and people who are different. People who like spaghetti like you, and those who like tuna fish sandwiches. People who like sports and people who prefer video games. You love all kinds of people.

That is who you are.

This is who you are:

strong
caring
leader
giving
just
loving
adventurous
creative
imaginative
happy
good
my boy

You are a strong boy, with a good heart, and this world needs more people like you.

For Contact:
WesleyDunn.com | instagram.com/wesdunn | twitter.com/wesdunn

Made in the USA
San Bernardino, CA
11 October 2017